Skip to My Lou

a traditional song
Illustrated by Debbie Tilley

HARCOURT BRACE & COMPANY

Orlando   Atlanta   Austin   Boston   San Francisco   Chicago   Dallas   New York
Toronto   London

Riding in a big bus,
Painted blue.

Good-bye to the city,
And school, too.

We're off to the farm!
Hurray! Ya-HOO!

Skip to my Lou, my darling!

Good morning, Farmer,
How are you?

Walk with your partners,
Two by two.

4

Don't get lost, or
What will we do?

Skip to my Lou, my darling!

Cows in the barnyard,
Moo, cows, moo.

Pigs, ducks, sheep,
And horses, too.

Hens and roosters,
Cock-a-doodle-do.

Skip to my Lou, my darling!

Close that gate,
And the barn door, too!

Look! All the animals
Are going through!

Oh, my goodness!
What did you do?

Skip to my Lou, my darling!

Cows in the farmhouse,
Shoo, cows, shoo!

Pigs, ducks, sheep,
And horses, too!

Hens and roosters!
What will we do?

Skip to my Lou, my darling!

Lou, Lou, skip to my Lou!
Lou, Lou, skip to my Lou!
Lou, Lou, skip to my Lou!
Skip to my Lou, my darling!
Whew!

Time to go now.
Toodle-oo!

But we're not sad,
And we're not blue—

Because next week, we're
GOING TO THE ZOO!

Skip to my Lou, my darling!

Printed in the United States of America

ISBN 0-15-307389-6

2 3 4 5 6 7 8 9 10   073   99   98   97